Discovering Vegan China

Rami Georgiev

Published by Rami Georgiev, 2023.

DISCOVERING VEGAN CHINA

First edition. February 5, 2023.

Copyright © 2023 Rami Georgiev.

ISBN: 979-8223612254

Written by Rami Georgiev.

Table of Contents

Dedicated to all the food lovers and travelers who seek to experience the world through the lens of their taste buds. This book is for those who believe that food is not just sustenance, but a way to connect with different cultures, people, and memories.

This book is also dedicated to all the vegans who are on a journey to live a more compassionate and healthier lifestyle, and who are constantly seeking new and exciting ways to enjoy delicious, plant-based meals.

And finally, this book is dedicated to the vibrant and diverse country of China, and to all the talented chefs, home cooks, and street vendors who have inspired us with their delicious and innovative vegan dishes. May this book serve as a tribute to their artistry and passion.

Thank you!

Rami Georgiev

Introduction

The growing popularity of veganism

IN RECENT YEARS, VEGANISM has gained significant attention and popularity as a lifestyle choice. With increased awareness about the impact of food choices on the environment, animal welfare, and health, many people are seeking out plant-based alternatives to traditional meat- and dairy-based diets. This trend is not limited to the Western world, but can also be seen in countries like China, where an increasing number of people are choosing to adopt a vegan lifestyle.

The unique challenges of veganism in China

WHILE THE CONCEPT OF veganism is becoming more well-known in China, it can still be challenging for vegans to find suitable options in a country where meat and dairy are such an integral part of traditional cuisine. Many restaurants and food stalls serve dishes that contain animal-based ingredients, making it difficult for vegans to dine out without having to make special requests or face limited options. Additionally, language barriers can make it challenging for travelers to communicate their dietary restrictions and find vegan-friendly options.

Purpose of the book

THIS BOOK AIMS TO PROVIDE a comprehensive guide to discovering the best of vegan cuisine in China. From exploring the unique culinary traditions of each region, to finding vegan-friendly restaurants, shopping for ingredients, and learning cooking techniques, you will have all the tools you need to enjoy a delicious and satisfying vegan experience in China. Whether you are a local or a traveler, this book will provide you with the information you need to make informed decisions about what to eat and how to cook while in China.

Overview of the book

THE BOOK BEGINS BY exploring traditional Chinese cuisine and its relationship with meat and dairy. You will learn about the common ingredients, cooking techniques, and regional influences that shape the cuisine in China. This will provide a foundation for understanding how veganism can fit into the larger culinary landscape.

The core of the book consists of regional recipes, showcasing the diversity and creativity of vegan cuisine in different parts of China. From the northern regions of Beijing and Shanghai, to the southern regions of Guangzhou and Sichuan, you will discover a wide range of delicious and easy-to-prepare dishes that showcase the best of vegan Chinese cuisine.

In addition to recipes, the book includes practical information about finding vegan-friendly restaurants, shopping for ingredients, and navigating the challenges of eating vegan in China. You will learn about essential ingredients for your pantry, as well as techniques for cooking common vegan dishes like stir-fry, steaming, and braising.

The book concludes with a comprehensive list of resources for further exploration, including cookbooks, online resources, travel tips, and local vegan communities. Whether you are a seasoned vegan or just starting out on your plant-based journey, this book provides everything you need to discover the best of vegan cuisine in China.

The Growing Popularity of Veganism in China

IN RECENT YEARS, VEGANISM has gained significant attention and popularity as a lifestyle choice. With increased awareness about the impact of food choices on the environment, animal welfare, and health, many people are seeking out plant-based alternatives to traditional meat- and dairy-based diets. This trend is not limited to the Western world, but can also be seen in countries like China, where an increasing number of people are choosing to adopt a vegan lifestyle.

Veganism has a long history in China, dating back to the philosophical and religious movements of ancient times. Many Chinese religious traditions, such as Buddhism and Taoism, emphasize compassion for all living beings and have inspired followers to adopt vegetarian diets. However, despite this historical precedent, veganism was not widely adopted in China until recent years, when a new generation of vegans began to emerge in response to global trends and increased access to information.

The growth of veganism in China can be attributed to several factors, including increased awareness of environmental and animal welfare issues, growing concern about personal health, and the rise of vegan-friendly food options. In recent years, the popularity of plant-based diets has been driven by a growing number of high-profile celebrities, influencers, and health experts who promote the benefits of a vegan lifestyle.

Social media has played a significant role in the growth of veganism in China. Platforms like WeChat and Douyin (TikTok) have provided a space for vegan activists, influencers, and advocates to spread information about the benefits of veganism, share recipes and resources, and connect with like-minded individuals. Social media has also helped to dispel misconceptions about veganism, making it more accessible and appealing to a wider audience.

The growth of veganism in China has also been accompanied by the emergence of vegan-friendly food options. In recent years, many restaurants, cafes, and supermarkets have started offering plant-based alternatives, making it easier for vegans to find suitable options. In addition, there has been a rise in the number of specialty vegan food stores, which provide a wide range of vegan ingredients, products, and prepared foods.

The growing popularity of veganism in China is a reflection of a larger global trend, driven by increased awareness of environmental and animal welfare issues, as well as growing concern about personal health.

With the emergence of vegan-friendly food options, the growth of social media, and the support of influential figures, veganism is becoming more accessible and appealing to a wider audience in China. Whether for ethical, environmental, or health reasons, the trend towards veganism is likely to continue to grow in China and around the world in the years to come.

Chapter 1: Understanding Traditional Chinese Cuisine

Traditional Chinese cuisine is an important part of the country's cultural heritage and a source of national pride. It is known for its diverse flavors, cooking techniques, and use of fresh ingredients. From steamed buns to hot pot and dumplings, Chinese food has captured the hearts and palates of people around the world. This chapter will provide a comprehensive overview of traditional Chinese cuisine, including its history, regional specialties, cooking techniques, and unique ingredients.

The History of Traditional Chinese Cuisine

Traditional Chinese cuisine has a rich and varied history, shaped by the country's diverse geography, cultural traditions, and religious practices. From the imperial banquets of the Ming Dynasty to the simple, hearty meals of the countryside, Chinese food has evolved over thousands of years to reflect the country's changing cultural landscape.

Regional Specialties

One of the defining characteristics of traditional Chinese cuisine is its regional diversity. Each region of China has its own unique culinary traditions, shaped by local ingredients, cooking techniques, and cultural influences. Whether it's the spicy flavors of Sichuan cuisine or the delicate flavors of Cantonese cuisine, traditional Chinese food is diverse and flavorful.

Cooking Techniques

Chinese cooking is known for its diverse and sophisticated techniques, which range from steaming and stir-frying to braising and roasting. Each cooking method has its own unique flavors and textures, and chefs are trained to use these techniques to bring out the best in their ingredients. Whether it's perfecting a stir-fry or mastering the art of dumpling-making, cooking traditional Chinese cuisine is a true art form.

Unique Ingredients

Traditional Chinese cuisine is known for its use of fresh, seasonal ingredients. From exotic mushrooms to flavorful herbs and spices, Chinese chefs use a wide variety of ingredients to create dishes that are both nutritious and delicious. This chapter will explore some of the unique ingredients that are essential to traditional Chinese cooking, including their flavors, textures, and nutritional benefits.

This chapter will provide a comprehensive overview of traditional Chinese cuisine, offering a deeper understanding of its history, regional specialties, cooking techniques, and unique ingredients. Whether you're a seasoned foodie or just a curious beginner, this chapter will provide a rich and delicious introduction to the world of traditional Chinese cuisine.

The role of meat and dairy in traditional dishes in Chinese cuisine

CHINESE CUISINE IS diverse and has a rich history that dates back thousands of years. One of the key components of traditional Chinese dishes is meat and dairy, which play a significant role in adding flavor, texture, and nutrition to the dishes.

One of the most common meats used in Chinese cuisine is pork, which is the main source of protein for many Chinese people. Pork is used in a variety of dishes, including stir-fries, stews, and dumplings, and is known for its versatility and rich flavor. In addition, beef and mutton are also used in traditional Chinese dishes, especially in northern China where these meats are more prevalent.

Dairy products are not as commonly used in Chinese cuisine as they are in Western cuisine, but they still play a role in certain dishes. For example, tofu, or bean curd, is made from soy milk and is a staple ingredient in many vegetarian dishes. It is also used as a meat substitute in dishes such as mapo tofu, which is a spicy dish made with tofu and ground meat.

Another dairy product that is used in Chinese cuisine is yogurt, which is commonly consumed as a snack or dessert. Yogurt is also used in savory dishes, such as the Sichuan dish known as "fish-fragrant yogurt." This dish is made with sliced fish that is marinated in yogurt, ginger, and garlic, then stir-fried with vegetables.

One of the most iconic traditional Chinese dishes that incorporates dairy is the hot pot. This is a communal dish that is typically enjoyed during the colder months and involves a pot of boiling broth that diners cook their own food in. The broth is often made with dairy, such as yogurt or cream, which adds richness and flavor to the dish.

In conclusion, meat and dairy play a significant role in traditional Chinese cuisine, adding flavor, texture, and nutrition to dishes. Pork is one of the most commonly used meats, while tofu and yogurt are among the dairy products used in Chinese cooking. These ingredients help to create the unique flavors and aromas that are characteristic of Chinese cuisine and make it a beloved cuisine around the world.

Common ingredients and cooking techniques

COMMON INGREDIENTS and cooking techniques in Chinese cuisine

Chinese cuisine is known for its rich and diverse flavors, and this is achieved through the use of a variety of ingredients and cooking techniques. In this chapter, we will explore some of the most common ingredients and cooking techniques used in traditional Chinese cuisine.

Ingredients:

Rice: Rice is a staple ingredient in Chinese cuisine and is used in a variety of dishes, including fried rice, congee, and stir-fried dishes.

Noodles: Noodles are another staple ingredient in Chinese cuisine and come in a range of shapes and sizes, including egg noodles, rice noodles, and cellophane noodles. Noodles are used in dishes such as lo mein and chow mein, and are often paired with vegetables and meats.

Soy Sauce: Soy sauce is a staple condiment in Chinese cuisine and is used to add flavor to dishes, as well as to marinate meats. Dark soy sauce is commonly used in dishes that require a rich, savory flavor, while light soy sauce is used in dishes that require a more delicate flavor.

Garlic and Ginger: Garlic and ginger are two of the most commonly used spices in Chinese cuisine and are used to add flavor and fragrance to dishes. These ingredients are often used in combination to create a fragrant base for stir-fries and soups.

Scallions: Scallions are a type of green onion that are widely used in Chinese cuisine to add flavor and fragrance to dishes. They are often used as a garnish, and are also used in stir-fries, soups, and sauces.

Cooking Techniques:

Stir-Frying: Stir-frying is one of the most commonly used cooking techniques in Chinese cuisine and involves quickly cooking ingredients in a hot wok over high heat. This technique allows ingredients to retain their texture and color, and is commonly used to cook vegetables and meats.

Braising: Braising is a slow-cooking technique that involves cooking ingredients in a flavorful liquid, such as a sauce or broth, over low heat for an extended period of time. This technique is often used to cook meats and vegetables, and results in tender and flavorful dishes.

Steaming: Steaming is a healthy and flavorful cooking technique that involves cooking ingredients in a steamer basket over boiling water. This technique is commonly used to cook fish, dumplings, and buns, and results in delicate and tender dishes.

Boiling: Boiling is a simple and effective cooking technique that involves cooking ingredients in boiling water. This technique is often used to cook noodles, dumplings, and soups, and results in soft and flavorful dishes.

In conclusion, Chinese cuisine relies on a combination of ingredients and cooking techniques to create its unique and flavorful dishes. Rice, noodles, soy sauce, garlic and ginger, and scallions are just a few of the ingredients that are commonly used in Chinese cooking. Stir-frying, braising, steaming, and boiling are just a few of the cooking techniques that are used to bring these ingredients to life. Whether you are a fan of spicy Sichuan dishes or delicate Cantonese cuisine, the combination of these ingredients and cooking techniques results in a wide range of delicious and flavorful dishes.

The influence of regional cuisine in Chinese cuisine

CHINA IS A VAST COUNTRY with a rich cultural heritage, and this is reflected in the diversity of its regional cuisines. Each region has its own unique culinary traditions and techniques that have been developed over centuries, and this has resulted in a wealth of delicious and flavorful dishes that are unique to each region. In this chapter, we will explore the influence of regional cuisine in Chinese cuisine and how it has helped to shape the flavors and ingredients that are used in traditional Chinese dishes.

Cantonese Cuisine: Cantonese cuisine is characterized by its light and delicate flavors, and is renowned for its seafood dishes. This region is located in southern China and is known for its use of fresh ingredients, such as fish, seafood, and vegetables, which are cooked with minimal seasoning to retain their natural flavors. Some of the most famous Cantonese dishes include dim sum, roasted pork, and steamed fish.

Sichuan Cuisine: Sichuan cuisine, also known as Szechuan cuisine, is characterized by its bold and spicy flavors. This region is located in southwestern China and is known for its use of Sichuan peppercorns, which add a unique numbing and spicy flavor to dishes. Some of the most famous Sichuan dishes include mapo tofu, kung pao chicken, and hot pot.

Hunan Cuisine: Hunan cuisine is characterized by its bold and spicy flavors, and is known for its use of chili peppers and other spices. This region is located in central China and is known for its hearty and flavorful dishes, such as steamed fish and spicy beef noodle soup.

Shandong Cuisine: Shandong cuisine is characterized by its use of bold flavors and simple cooking techniques, and is known for its use of seafood and vegetables. This region is located in northeastern China and is known for its seafood dishes, such as stir-fried clams and braised sea cucumber.

Jiangsu Cuisine: Jiangsu cuisine is characterized by its light and delicate flavors, and is known for its use of seafood and freshwater ingredients. This region is located in eastern China and is known for its sophisticated dishes, such as braised abalone and steamed eel.

Each of these regional cuisines has its own unique flavors and ingredients, and has had a significant influence on the development of traditional Chinese cuisine. The combination of these regional cuisines has created a diverse and flavorful culinary tradition that is enjoyed by people all over the world. Whether you prefer the bold and spicy flavors of Sichuan cuisine or the light and delicate flavors of Cantonese cuisine, the influence of regional cuisine in Chinese cuisine has resulted in a wide range of delicious and flavorful dishes that are sure to delight your taste buds.

Chapter 2: Regional Vegan Recipes

Chinese cuisine is known for its rich and diverse culinary traditions, and its use of a variety of ingredients and cooking techniques to create flavorful and delicious dishes. While meat and dairy have traditionally played a significant role in Chinese cooking, there is also a wealth of regional vegan recipes that have been developed over centuries, making use of fresh vegetables, grains, and legumes to create delicious and nutritious meals. In this chapter, we will explore the influence of regional cuisine in Chinese vegan cooking, and examine some of the most popular and beloved regional vegan recipes that are enjoyed by people all over the world. Whether you are a vegan or simply looking for a healthier and more plant-based way of eating, these regional vegan recipes offer a delicious and nutritious way to enjoy the flavors of traditional Chinese cuisine.

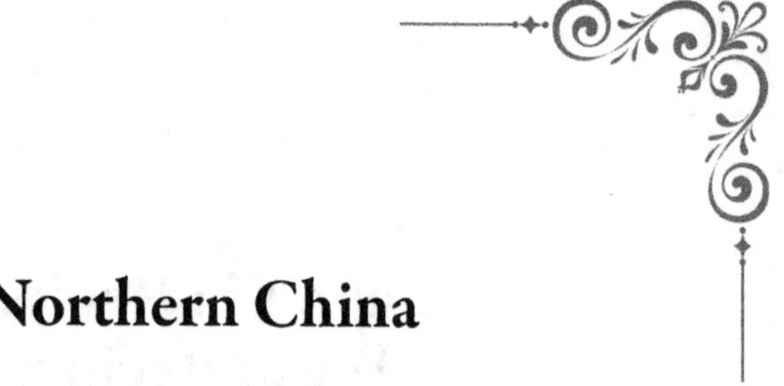

Northern China

Northern China is renowned for its rich and diverse culinary culture, characterized by hearty, savory dishes that make use of local ingredients and traditional cooking techniques. While meat and dairy are staple ingredients in many northern Chinese recipes, there is a growing trend towards veganism in this region, as more and more people seek to incorporate plant-based foods into their diets for health, ethical, or environmental reasons.

In this chapter, we will introduce you to some of the best vegan recipes from Northern China. From flavorful stir-fries to hearty soups and stews, these dishes will showcase the unique and delicious flavors of this region while also providing a nourishing and satisfying meal for those following a vegan lifestyle. So whether you are a seasoned vegan, or simply looking to try something new, we invite you to explore these delicious Northern Chinese vegan recipes and discover the flavors of this fascinating region.

Beijing-style vegetable noodles are a classic dish that combines the tenderness of fresh noodles with the crunch and flavor of a variety of vegetables. This easy-to-make recipe is both filling and healthy, making it a great option for a quick lunch or dinner.

Beijing-style vegetable noodles

INGREDIENTS:

    8 oz fresh egg noodles
    2 tbsp oil
    2 cloves of garlic, minced
    1 medium carrot, julienned
    1 small bell pepper, sliced
    1/2 cup cabbage, shredded
    1/2 cup bean sprouts
    2 scallions, sliced
    2 tbsp soy sauce
    1 tsp sugar
    Salt and pepper to taste

Instructions:

Cook the egg noodles in a large pot of boiling salted water for about 2-3 minutes or until al dente. Drain and rinse with cold water to stop the cooking process. Set aside.

In a large wok or frying pan, heat the oil over high heat. Add the garlic and stir-fry for 30 seconds.

Add the carrots, bell pepper, cabbage, and bean sprouts to the pan and stir-fry for another 2-3 minutes or until the vegetables are just tender.

Add the cooked noodles to the pan and toss to combine with the vegetables.

Stir in the soy sauce, sugar, salt, and pepper, and continue to stir-fry for another minute or until everything is well combined.

Serve the Beijing-style vegetable noodles hot, garnished with sliced scallions.

Enjoy this delicious and nutritious dish, inspired by the flavors of Northern China!

Jiaozi (dumplings) with a vegan filling

INGREDIENTS:

2 cups all-purpose flour

1/2 cup warm water

2 tbsp vegetable oil

1 tsp salt

1 tbsp cornstarch

For the filling:

2 cups finely chopped cabbage

1 cup finely chopped mushrooms

1/2 cup grated carrots

1/2 cup chopped scallions

2 cloves of garlic, minced

1 tbsp grated ginger

2 tbsp soy sauce

1 tsp sesame oil

Salt and pepper to taste

Instructions:

In a large bowl, mix the flour, salt, cornstarch, vegetable oil, and warm water until a dough forms.

Knead the dough for several minutes until it is smooth and elastic. Cover with plastic wrap and let it rest for 30 minutes.

In a large pan, heat 1 tbsp of vegetable oil and sauté the garlic and ginger until fragrant.

Add the chopped cabbage, mushrooms, carrots, and scallions to the pan and cook until softened, about 5-7 minutes.

Season the filling with soy sauce, sesame oil, salt, and pepper, and let it cool completely.

Divide the dough into golf ball-sized pieces and roll each into a thin circle.

Place a spoonful of the filling into the center of each dough circle.

Pinch the edges of the dough to seal and form a dumpling.

Repeat with the remaining dough and filling.

In a large pot of boiling water, cook the dumplings for 3-5 minutes until they float to the surface. Serve with soy sauce or vinegar for dipping. Enjoy!

Eastern China

Eastern Chinese cuisine is a rich and diverse culinary tradition, renowned for its delicate flavors and intricate cooking techniques. While meat-based dishes are a staple in many parts of Eastern China, there are also a variety of delicious and satisfying vegan options available. From stir-fried vegetables to soups and stews, Eastern China has a wealth of plant-based dishes that are both nutritious and delicious. Whether you're a long-time vegan or simply looking to incorporate more plant-based options into your diet, Eastern Chinese cuisine offers an array of options that are sure to please. So why not explore this vibrant and flavorful culinary tradition today, and discover the delicious world of Eastern Chinese vegan cuisine!

Shanghai-style braised eggplant

INGREDIENTS:

2 large eggplants, cut into 1 inch pieces

1 medium onion, chopped

2 cloves of garlic, minced

1 tbsp grated ginger

1 red bell pepper, chopped

1 tbsp fermented black beans, rinsed and drained

1 tbsp hoisin sauce

1 tbsp soy sauce

2 tsp sugar

1 tsp cornstarch

2 tbsp vegetable oil

1 cup vegetable broth

1 tsp sesame oil

2 tbsp chopped scallions for garnish

Instructions:

In a small bowl, mix together the hoisin sauce, soy sauce, sugar, and cornstarch. Set aside.

In a large pan or wok, heat the vegetable oil over medium-high heat. Add the eggplant and cook until softened and lightly browned, about 5 minutes.

Remove the eggplant from the pan and set aside.

In the same pan, add the onion, garlic, ginger, red bell pepper, and fermented black beans. Cook until the vegetables are softened, about 3-5 minutes.

Return the eggplant to the pan and stir in the sauce mixture.

Add the vegetable broth to the pan and bring the mixture to a boil.

Reduce the heat to low, cover the pan, and simmer until the eggplant is fully cooked and the sauce has thickened, about 10-15 minutes.

Stir in the sesame oil.

Serve the braised eggplant over rice, garnished with chopped scallions. Enjoy!

Sticky rice balls with sweet filling

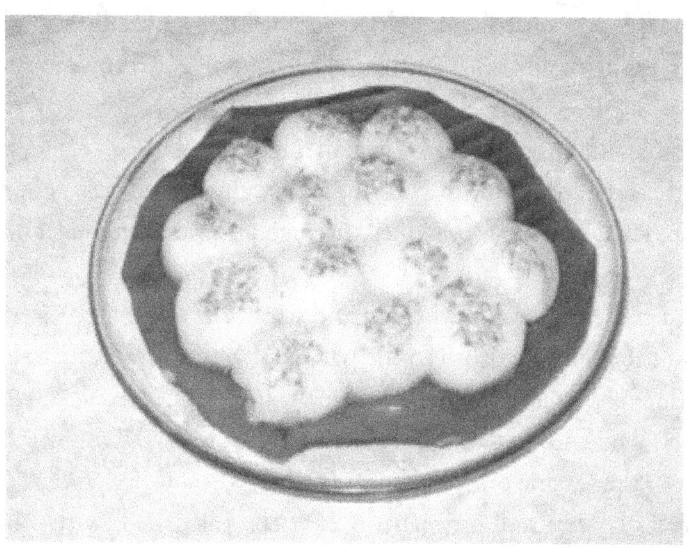

INGREDIENTS:

    2 cups glutinous rice flour

    1 cup warm water

    1/4 tsp salt

    1 tbsp vegetable oil

    For the filling:

    1 cup sweet red bean paste

    1 cup finely chopped peanuts

    1/2 cup chopped coconut flakes

    1/4 cup sugar

Instructions:

In a large bowl, mix the glutinous rice flour, salt, and warm water until a dough forms.

Knead the dough for several minutes until it is smooth and no longer sticky. Divide the dough into golf ball-sized pieces.

In a separate bowl, mix the red bean paste, peanuts, coconut flakes, and sugar to make the filling.

Flatten each dough piece into a circle, place a spoonful of the filling in the center, and pinch the edges to seal the dough around the filling.

Roll the sticky rice ball into a smooth ball. Repeat with the remaining dough and filling.

Boil a pot of water and carefully add the sticky rice balls to the boiling water. Cook for 5-7 minutes, until they float to the surface.

Remove the sticky rice balls from the water and let them cool slightly. Serve warm or at room temperature. Enjoy!

Southern China

Southern Chinese cuisine is known for its diverse array of flavors and ingredients, incorporating a variety of plant-based dishes that are both nutritious and delicious. With a focus on fresh vegetables and flavorful sauces, Southern Chinese vegan cuisine offers a wide range of options for those seeking meat-free meals. From spicy stir-fries to savory soups and stews, Southern Chinese cuisine is a celebration of the abundance and variety of plant-based ingredients. Whether you're a lifelong vegan or simply looking to incorporate more plant-based options into your diet, Southern Chinese cuisine has something to offer. So why not explore this vibrant and flavorful culinary tradition today and discover the delicious world of Southern Chinese vegan cuisine!

Guangzhou-style steamed tofu with vegetables

INGREDIENTS:

1 block firm tofu, sliced into 1/2-inch pieces

2 cups mixed vegetables of your choice (such as sliced carrots, bell peppers, mushrooms, and snap peas)

2 cloves of garlic, minced

1 tbsp grated ginger

2 tbsp soy sauce

1 tbsp sesame oil

2 tbsp vegetable oil

1 tbsp cornstarch

1/4 cup water

2 tbsp chopped scallions for garnish

Instructions:

In a small bowl, mix together the soy sauce, sesame oil, vegetable oil, cornstarch, and water. Set aside.

In a large steamer, place the sliced tofu in a single layer.

In a separate steamer basket, place the mixed vegetables.

Steam both the tofu and vegetables for 5-7 minutes, until the vegetables are slightly softened and the tofu is heated through.

In a large pan or wok, heat 2 tablespoons of vegetable oil over medium-high heat. Add the garlic and ginger and cook until fragrant, about 1 minute.

Add the steamed vegetables to the pan and stir-fry for 2-3 minutes, until they are coated in the garlic and ginger mixture.

Stir in the sauce mixture and cook until the sauce has thickened, about 2-3 minutes.

Place the steamed tofu in a serving dish and top with the vegetable mixture.

Garnish with chopped scallions. Serve immediately. Enjoy!

Fried rice with mushrooms and vegetables

INGREDIENTS:

2 cups cooked white rice, chilled

1 cup mixed mushrooms (such as shiitake, oyster, and button), sliced

1 cup mixed vegetables of your choice (such as diced carrots, bell peppers, and peas)

2 cloves of garlic, minced

1 tbsp grated ginger

2 tbsp soy sauce

2 tbsp vegetable oil

2 beaten eggs (optional)

2 tbsp chopped scallions for garnish

Instructions:

In a large pan or wok, heat 1 tablespoon of vegetable oil over medium-high heat. Add the beaten eggs, if using, and scramble until set. Remove from the pan and set aside.

In the same pan, heat another tablespoon of vegetable oil. Add the garlic and ginger and cook until fragrant, about 1 minute.

Add the sliced mushrooms and stir-fry for 2-3 minutes, until they are tender and lightly browned.

Add the mixed vegetables to the pan and stir-fry for 2-3 minutes, until they are slightly softened.

Stir in the cooked rice and soy sauce, breaking up any clumps of rice with a spatula.

Stir in the scrambled eggs, if using, and cook until the rice is evenly coated in the sauce and heated through.

Garnish with chopped scallions. Serve immediately. Enjoy!

Western China

Western China is a region with a rich and diverse culinary tradition, featuring a wide range of plant-based dishes that are both flavorful and nutritious. From spicy stir-fries to hearty stews and soups, Western Chinese vegan cuisine offers a world of flavor and variety to those seeking meat-free meals. With a focus on fresh ingredients and bold spices, Western Chinese vegan cuisine is a celebration of the abundant bounty of plant-based foods. Whether you're a lifelong vegan or simply looking to add more plant-based options to your diet, Western Chinese cuisine has something to offer. So join us as we explore the exciting and delicious world of Western Chinese vegan cuisine and discover the many delicious and satisfying dishes that this region has to offer!

Sichuan-style spicy tofu

INGREDIENTS:

 1 block firm tofu, sliced into 1-inch cubes

 1 red bell pepper, sliced

 1 green bell pepper, sliced

 1 small onion, sliced

 4 cloves of garlic, minced

 1 tbsp grated ginger

 2 tbsp Sichuan peppercorns

 2 tbsp vegetable oil

 2 tbsp chili paste

 2 tbsp soy sauce

 2 tbsp sugar

 1/4 cup water

 2 tbsp chopped scallions for garnish

Instructions:

In a large pan or wok, heat the vegetable oil over medium-high heat.
Add the Sichuan peppercorns and stir-fry for 30 seconds, until fragrant.
Add the garlic and ginger and cook until fragrant, about 1 minute.

Add the sliced bell peppers, onion, and tofu and stir-fry for 3-5 minutes, until the vegetables are slightly softened and the tofu is lightly browned.

In a small bowl, mix together the chili paste, soy sauce, sugar, and water. Stir into the pan.

Cook until the sauce has thickened, about 2-3 minutes.

Garnish with chopped scallions. Serve immediately. Enjoy!

Hand-pulled noodles with mushroom sauce

INGREDIENTS:

2 cups all-purpose flour

1 tsp salt

1 tsp vegetable oil

1/2 cup warm water

1 cup sliced mixed mushrooms (such as shiitake, oyster, and button)

2 cloves of garlic, minced

1 tbsp grated ginger

2 tbsp vegetable oil

1/2 cup vegetable broth

2 tbsp soy sauce

2 tbsp cornstarch mixed with 2 tbsp water

2 tbsp chopped scallions for garnish

Instructions:

In a large bowl, mix together the flour, salt, and 1 tsp of vegetable oil until well combined. Gradually add the warm water, kneading the mixture until it forms a smooth and elastic dough. Cover the dough and let it rest for 30 minutes.

In a separate pan, heat 2 tablespoons of vegetable oil over medium-high heat. Add the garlic and ginger and cook until fragrant, about 1 minute.

Add the sliced mushrooms and stir-fry for 2-3 minutes, until they are tender and lightly browned.

Stir in the vegetable broth, soy sauce, and cornstarch mixture. Cook until the sauce has thickened, about 2-3 minutes.

On a lightly floured surface, divide the dough into 4 equal portions. Roll each portion into a long and thin rope, about 1/2 inch in diameter. Using your hands, gently stretch and pull each rope into long, thin noodles.

Boil a large pot of salted water. Add the noodles to the pot and cook for 2-3 minutes, until they are tender and cooked through.

Serve the cooked noodles topped with the mushroom sauce and garnished with chopped scallions. Enjoy!

Chapter 3: Finding Vegan-Friendly Restaurants

Dining out can be a challenge for vegans, especially when navigating unfamiliar menus. However, finding vegan-friendly restaurants has become easier in recent years, with more and more eateries offering plant-based options. In this chapter, we'll provide tips and tricks for finding restaurants that cater to your dietary needs, as well as some of our favorite vegan-friendly spots. Whether you're traveling or simply looking to try something new, we'll help you find the best places to enjoy delicious, cruelty-free meals. So let's get started and discover the many wonderful vegan-friendly restaurants that are waiting for you!

Major cities with vegan communities in China

CHINA IS A VAST AND diverse country, with many different cities offering unique cultural and culinary experiences. For vegans, this can be both exciting and overwhelming, as each city presents its own unique challenges and opportunities. To help you navigate the plant-based scene in China, here is a closer look at some of the major cities with thriving vegan communities.

Shanghai: Shanghai is one of the largest cities in China, and it is also one of the most vegan-friendly. With a growing number of vegetarian and vegan restaurants, Shanghai offers a wide variety of options for those following a plant-based diet. From traditional Chinese vegetarian dishes to international cuisine, there is something for everyone in Shanghai. Some popular vegan-friendly restaurants in Shanghai include Pure Lotus, a upscale vegetarian restaurant serving traditional Chinese dishes with a modern twist, and Lotus Eatery, a cozy restaurant that offers a variety of vegan options, including mock meat dishes and fresh salads.

Beijing: Beijing is the capital city of China, and it is also home to a growing number of vegan-friendly restaurants. From street food stalls to upscale dining establishments, Beijing offers a wide range of options for vegans. Some of the most popular vegan-friendly restaurants in Beijing include Loving Hut, a chain of vegan restaurants that offer a variety of international dishes, and The Veggie Table, a upscale vegetarian restaurant serving a variety of vegetarian and vegan dishes.

Guangzhou: Guangzhou is a city known for its rich food culture, and it is also home to a thriving vegan community. With a growing number of vegetarian and vegan restaurants, Guangzhou offers a wide range of options for those following a plant-based diet. Some popular vegan-friendly restaurants in Guangzhou include Vegan House, a cozy vegan restaurant serving traditional Chinese dishes with a vegan twist, and Veggie Corner, a vegan café that offers a variety of fresh and healthy plant-based options.

Shenzhen: Shenzhen is a city located in the southern part of China, and it is also home to a thriving vegan community. With a growing number of vegetarian and vegan restaurants, Shenzhen offers a wide range of options for those following a plant-based diet. Some popular vegan-friendly restaurants in Shenzhen include Green Common, a vegan restaurant and grocery store that offers a variety of international and Chinese-style dishes, and Veggie SF, a vegan restaurant serving plant-based burgers and other comfort food favorites.

These are just a few of the many cities in China with thriving vegan communities. Whether you are traveling or simply looking to try something new, these cities offer a wide variety of options for those following a plant-based diet. From traditional Chinese dishes to international cuisine, there is something for everyone in China's vegan-friendly cities. So whether you are looking to indulge in delicious plant-based meals or simply to connect with like-minded individuals, these cities offer the perfect destination for anyone looking to explore the world of veganism in China.

Tips for identifying vegan-friendly options on menus in China

DINING OUT AS A VEGAN in China can be a challenge, especially if you are unfamiliar with the local cuisine. However, with a few simple tips, you can easily identify vegan-friendly options on menus and enjoy delicious plant-based meals. Here are some key things to keep in mind when dining out in China:

Look for vegetarian restaurants: The easiest way to find vegan-friendly options is to look for restaurants that cater specifically to vegetarians. Many vegetarian restaurants in China offer a variety of vegan options, including traditional Chinese dishes made with mock meats and tofu, as well as fresh salads and stir-fry dishes.

Use translation apps: Many menu items in China are written in Mandarin, so it can be helpful to have a translation app on hand. Simply take a photo of the menu, and the app will provide an English translation, making it easier to identify vegan-friendly options.

Know the keywords: When searching for vegan-friendly options, it is helpful to know the key words to look for. Some common terms used to describe vegan dishes in China include "tofu" (□□), "stir-fry vegetables" (□□□), and "vegetarian" (□□).

Ask the waiter: If you are still unsure about the ingredients in a dish, simply ask the waiter for help. Most restaurant staff in China are familiar with vegetarianism and will be able to tell you if a dish contains any animal products.

Avoid dishes that contain egg or dairy: Some dishes in China may contain egg or dairy, even if they do not contain meat. To ensure that your meal is completely vegan, avoid dishes that contain these ingredients, such as omelets, soups, and sauces.

Try street food stalls: Street food stalls are a popular dining option in China, and many of them offer a variety of vegan-friendly options. From steamed buns filled with tofu and vegetables to spicy noodle dishes, street food stalls are a great place to try new vegan dishes and get a taste of the local cuisine.

By following these simple tips, you can easily identify vegan-friendly options on menus and enjoy delicious plant-based meals while dining out in China. Whether you are looking for traditional Chinese dishes or international cuisine, there is something for everyone in China's vibrant and growing vegan community. So why not explore the many delicious and vegan-friendly options that are waiting for you in China today!

Popular vegan restaurant chains in China

CHINA HAS A THRIVING vegan community, and there are many popular vegan restaurant chains that cater to the growing demand for plant-based cuisine. Whether you are in the mood for traditional Chinese dishes or international cuisine, there is a vegan restaurant chain in China that will suit your tastes. Here are some of the most popular vegan restaurant chains in China:

Vegetarian Lifestyle (◇◇◇◇) - Vegetarian Lifestyle is a chain of vegetarian restaurants that serves a variety of vegan dishes, including traditional Chinese dishes made with mock meats and tofu, as well as international cuisine. With locations in major cities throughout China, Vegetarian Lifestyle is a great option for vegans who are looking for a convenient and delicious meal.

Loving Hut (◇◇◇◇) - Loving Hut is a popular vegan restaurant chain with locations in cities throughout China, including Beijing, Shanghai, and Guangzhou. Offering a range of vegan dishes, from stir-fry dishes and soups to sweet and savory snacks, Loving Hut is a great option for vegans who are looking for a quick and affordable meal.

Green Common (◇◇◇◇) - Green Common is a chain of vegetarian restaurants that offers a variety of vegan options, including dishes made with mock meats and tofu, as well as salads, smoothies, and snacks. With locations in cities throughout China, Green Common is a great option for vegans who are looking for a healthy and convenient meal.

The Veggie Table (◇◇◇) - The Veggie Table is a chain of vegan restaurants that offers a variety of vegan dishes, including traditional Chinese dishes made with mock meats and tofu, as well as international cuisine. With locations in cities throughout China, The Veggie Table is a great option for vegans who are looking for a delicious and affordable meal.

The Herbivorous Butcher (◇◇◇◇) - The Herbivorous Butcher is a chain of vegan restaurants that offers a variety of vegan dishes, including traditional Chinese dishes made with mock meats and tofu, as well as international cuisine. With locations in cities throughout China, The Herbivorous Butcher is a great option for vegans who are looking for a delicious and innovative meal.

These are just a few of the popular vegan restaurant chains in China. Whether you are in the mood for a quick snack or a full-course meal, these restaurants offer a variety of vegan-friendly options that are sure to satisfy. So why not explore the many delicious and vegan-friendly options that are waiting for you in China today!

Chapter 4: Shopping for Vegan Ingredients

Shopping for vegan ingredients can be a challenge in any country, but in China, it can be especially challenging due to the language barrier and unfamiliar products. However, with a little research and some insider tips, it is possible to find all of the ingredients you need to prepare delicious and healthy vegan meals. In this chapter, we will explore the best places to shop for vegan ingredients in China, as well as offer tips for identifying vegan-friendly products and navigating the grocery store. Whether you are a seasoned vegan or new to the lifestyle, this chapter will provide you with the information and resources you need to make your shopping experience as easy and enjoyable as possible.

Understanding label language in China

WHEN SHOPPING FOR VEGAN ingredients in China, it is important to understand the language on food labels in order to make informed purchasing decisions. The language on food labels in China can be different from what you are used to in your home country, and it is important to be aware of the key terms and symbols that indicate whether a product is vegan or not.

Here are some key terms and symbols to look for on food labels in China:

◇ (sù) - This character means "vegetarian" and indicates that a product is suitable for vegans.

◇◇ (hán rǔ) - This phrase means "contains milk" and is used to indicate that a product contains dairy.

◇◇ (hán dàn) - This phrase means "contains egg" and is used to indicate that a product contains eggs.

◇◇ (hán yú) - This phrase means "contains fish" and is used to indicate that a product contains fish.

◇◇ (hán ròu) - This phrase means "contains meat" and is used to indicate that a product contains meat.

◇◇◇ (shí yòng yóu) - This phrase means "cooking oil" and is used to indicate the type of oil used in a product. It is important to look for products that use vegetable oil instead of animal-derived oils such as lard or tallow.

◇◇◇◇◇◇◇ (sù shí zhǔ yì zhě zhuān yòng) - This phrase means "for vegetarian use only" and indicates that a product is suitable for vegans.

◇◇◇ (dòng wù yóu) - This phrase means "animal oil" and is used to indicate that a product contains animal-derived oil.

◇◇ (nǎi lào) - This word means "cheese" and is used to indicate that a product contains dairy.

It is also important to note that some products may contain animal-derived ingredients that are not listed on the label, such as gelatin or honey. In these cases, it is a good idea to do some research and familiarize yourself with common animal-derived ingredients and how they are made.

In conclusion, understanding label language in China is crucial for vegans who want to make informed purchasing decisions. By familiarizing yourself with key terms and symbols, you can ensure that you are purchasing vegan-friendly products and avoid accidentally consuming animal-derived ingredients. With a little research and attention to detail, shopping for vegan ingredients in China can be a simple and enjoyable experience.

Essential vegan pantry items in China cuisine

A WELL-STOCKED PANTRY is essential for creating delicious and authentic Chinese-style vegan dishes at home. In Chinese cuisine, there are several staple ingredients that are used frequently and are important to have on hand in order to create a variety of different dishes. Whether you are a seasoned vegan cook or new to Chinese-style cooking, having these ingredients on hand will make meal planning and preparation much easier and more enjoyable.

Here is a list of essential vegan pantry items for Chinese cuisine:

Soy sauce - A staple in Chinese cooking, soy sauce is used to add saltiness and umami flavor to dishes. Look for a high-quality, low-sodium variety for best results.

Rice vinegar - This mild-tasting vinegar is commonly used in Chinese cooking to add tanginess and balance flavors.

Sesame oil - Made from toasted sesame seeds, this oil has a nutty flavor and is used as a condiment or for cooking.

Shaoxing wine - A type of rice wine, this is a common ingredient in Chinese cooking used to add depth of flavor to dishes.

Ginger - Fresh ginger root adds a pungent and slightly sweet flavor to Chinese dishes, and is used both in cooking and as a condiment.

Garlic - Used frequently in Chinese cooking, garlic adds depth of flavor and is used both in cooking and as a condiment.

Chinese five-spice powder - A blend of spices that typically includes cinnamon, cloves, fennel seed, star anise, and peppercorns, Chinese five-spice powder adds depth of flavor to dishes and is commonly used in savory and sweet recipes.

Star anise - A star-shaped spice commonly used in Chinese cooking, star anise adds a sweet and licorice-like flavor to dishes.

Chilies - Fresh or dried chilies add heat and flavor to Chinese dishes, and can be used to adjust the spiciness to your taste.

Bean paste - Made from fermented soybeans, bean paste is commonly used in Chinese cooking to add depth of flavor and umami to dishes.

Rice noodles - Rice noodles are a staple in Chinese cuisine and are used in a variety of dishes, including stir-fries, soups, and salads.

Tofu - Made from soybeans, tofu is a versatile and nutritious ingredient that is commonly used in Chinese cooking.

Rice - Rice is a staple in Chinese cuisine and is used as a base for many dishes, including stir-fries, soups, and rice bowls.

Vegetables - A variety of fresh vegetables, such as bok choy, snow peas, mushrooms, and bell peppers, are commonly used in Chinese cooking to add flavor and nutrition to dishes.

By keeping these essential vegan pantry items on hand, you will be able to create a variety of delicious and authentic Chinese-style vegan dishes with ease. Whether you are looking to make classic dishes like mapo tofu or something new, these ingredients will help you to bring the flavors of China into your kitchen.

Finding specialty vegan stores

FINDING SPECIALTY VEGAN stores in China can be a great way to access a wide variety of vegan ingredients and products, as well as get inspiration for new recipes and cooking ideas. Whether you are a long-time vegan or new to the lifestyle, shopping at a specialty store can be a fun and enjoyable experience, as well as a great way to support the vegan community in China.

Here are a few tips for finding specialty vegan stores in China:

Research online - Use search engines, social media, and online vegan forums to find information about specialty vegan stores in your area. You can also reach out to local vegan groups and organizations for recommendations.

Check out food markets - Food markets, such as wet markets and supermarkets, are a great place to start your search for specialty vegan stores. Look for stores that specialize in vegan products, or that have a large selection of vegan-friendly ingredients.

Visit specialty health food stores - Many health food stores carry a wide variety of vegan products, including snacks, meat alternatives, and plant-based milk. Ask the staff for recommendations, and keep an eye out for stores that specialize in vegan products.

Look for online vegan stores - Shopping online is a convenient way to access a wide variety of vegan products, including ingredients, snacks, and other specialty items. Be sure to check out online vegan stores that cater specifically to Chinese customers.

Check out local vegan festivals and events - Vegan festivals and events are a great place to connect with other vegans, sample new products, and find out about local specialty vegan stores.

When shopping at a specialty vegan store, be sure to look for products that are made from high-quality, natural ingredients and are free from artificial preservatives, flavors, and colors. You may also want to look for stores that offer a wide selection of vegan products, including snacks, meat alternatives, dairy alternatives, and other specialty items.

Shopping at a specialty vegan store can be a great way to support the vegan community in China, as well as access a wide variety of high-quality, plant-based products. Whether you are a seasoned vegan or new to the lifestyle, visiting a specialty vegan store is a great way to get inspired and try new products.

Chapter 5: Vegan Substitutions for Traditional Ingredients

Chinese cuisine is known for its rich flavors and diverse ingredients. However, for vegans, many traditional ingredients used in Chinese cooking can present a challenge. This chapter will provide information on substitutes for animal-based ingredients in Chinese cuisine to help make your cooking experience easier and more enjoyable. Whether you are making dishes like dumplings, stir-fries, or soups, there are a variety of plant-based options available that can mimic the taste and texture of meat and dairy. With these substitutes, you can create delicious and authentic-tasting vegan Chinese dishes that everyone can enjoy.

Replacing meat and dairy

FOR MANY PEOPLE, CHINESE cuisine is known for its rich flavors and diverse ingredients, including meat and dairy products. However, for those following a vegan diet, these ingredients can present a challenge. But with the right substitutes, it's possible to enjoy all the flavors and textures of Chinese cuisine without relying on meat or dairy products.

In this chapter, we'll explore the best alternatives to meat and dairy products that can be used to create delicious and authentic-tasting vegan Chinese dishes. From plant-based protein options like tofu and tempeh to non-dairy milk alternatives like almond milk and soy milk, we'll provide all the information you need to replace these ingredients in your favorite Chinese dishes.

Tofu and other plant-based protein options:

Tofu is a staple in vegan Chinese cooking and can be used to replace meat in dishes like stir-fries, soups, and stews. Tofu has a neutral flavor that makes it easy to absorb the flavors of the sauces and spices used in Chinese cooking. Additionally, it has a meat-like texture that makes it a great substitute for meat.

Other plant-based protein options include tempeh, seitan, and textured vegetable protein (TVP). These ingredients can be used to create vegan versions of traditional Chinese dishes like kung pao chicken and mapo tofu.

Non-dairy milk alternatives:

In Chinese cuisine, dairy is used in dishes like sweet soups and creamy sauces. Non-dairy milk alternatives like almond milk, soy milk, and coconut milk can be used to replace dairy milk in these dishes. These non-dairy milk options have a creamy texture that can mimic the texture of dairy milk, making them perfect for creating vegan versions of traditional Chinese desserts.

When using non-dairy milk alternatives in Chinese cooking, it is important to consider the flavor profile of the milk. For example, coconut milk has a distinct flavor that may not be suitable for all dishes. Almond milk and soy milk are more neutral in flavor, making them a better choice for dishes that require a milder flavor.

Overall, replacing meat and dairy in Chinese cuisine can be easily done with a variety of plant-based protein options and non-dairy milk alternatives. With these substitutes, you can create delicious and authentic-tasting vegan Chinese dishes that everyone can enjoy.

Using Plant-Based Ingredients in Traditional Chinese Dishes

CHINESE CUISINE HAS a rich and diverse history, with a wide range of traditional dishes that have been enjoyed for centuries. While many of these dishes were originally made with meat and dairy, it's now possible to recreate them using plant-based ingredients. This not only opens up Chinese cuisine to vegans and those with dietary restrictions, but it also offers new and exciting flavor combinations for everyone to enjoy.

Here are some popular traditional Chinese dishes and how to make them using plant-based ingredients:

Mapo Tofu: This classic Sichuan dish is typically made with ground beef and fermented bean paste. To make it vegan, simply replace the beef with crumbled tofu and the fermented bean paste with a vegan alternative.

Kung Pao Chicken: This spicy stir-fry dish is made with diced chicken, peanuts, and vegetables. To make it vegan, simply replace the chicken with diced tofu or tempeh and use a vegan alternative for any oyster sauce or other non-vegan ingredients.

Sweet and Sour Pork: This dish is traditionally made with breaded and fried pork that's stir-fried with a sweet and sour sauce. To make it vegan, replace the pork with breaded and fried tofu or tempeh.

Vegetable Dumplings: Dumplings are a staple of Chinese cuisine, and there are countless variations. To make a vegan version, simply fill the dumplings with a mixture of chopped vegetables, such as mushrooms, carrots, and bok choy.

Vegetable Stir-Fry: Stir-fry is one of the quickest and easiest ways to enjoy a variety of plant-based ingredients. Simply sauté your favorite vegetables, such as broccoli, bell peppers, and carrots, in a flavorful sauce.

In addition to these traditional dishes, there are many other ways to use plant-based ingredients in Chinese cuisine. From soups and broths to stir-fries and steamed dishes, the possibilities are virtually endless. The key is to experiment with different ingredients and flavor combinations until you find the ones that work best for you.

By incorporating plant-based ingredients into traditional Chinese dishes, you can enjoy all the flavors and textures you love while also following a vegan diet. So go ahead, get creative in the kitchen, and see what delicious plant-based dishes you can come up with!

Chapter 6: Travel Tips for a Vegan in China

Traveling as a vegan in China can be a unique and exciting experience, but it also requires some extra planning and preparation to ensure that you have access to adequate food options. In this guide, we will provide tips and information to help you make the most of your travels in China while staying true to your vegan lifestyle.

Communicating Vegan Needs

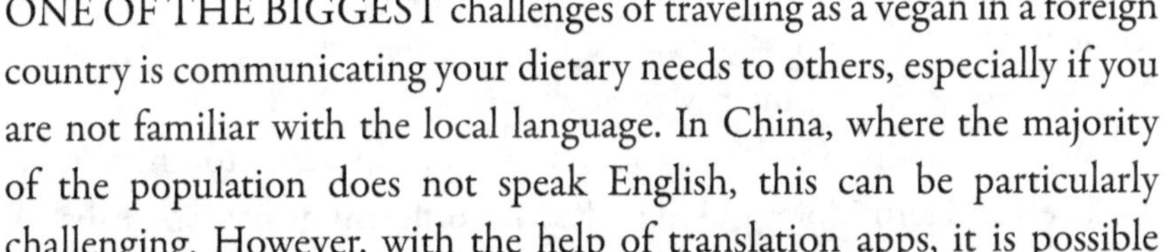

ONE OF THE BIGGEST challenges of traveling as a vegan in a foreign country is communicating your dietary needs to others, especially if you are not familiar with the local language. In China, where the majority of the population does not speak English, this can be particularly challenging. However, with the help of translation apps, it is possible to overcome the language barrier and ensure that you can communicate your vegan needs effectively.

Use of Translation Apps:

Translation apps are a valuable tool for vegan travelers in China, as they allow you to quickly and easily translate text, menus, and labels. Some popular translation apps include Google Translate, iTranslate, and Microsoft Translator. These apps use your smartphone's camera to scan text and translate it into the language of your choice. They can also be used to translate speech in real-time, making it easier to communicate with locals.

When using a translation app, it is important to keep in mind that the translations may not always be 100% accurate, so it is always a good idea to double-check the translations before relying on them. Additionally, some translation apps have limitations with languages such as Chinese, which can have multiple characters with different meanings, so it is important to exercise caution and use common sense when relying on these tools.

Key Phrases for Vegan Travelers:

In addition to using a translation app, it is also helpful to learn a few key phrases in Chinese that can be used to communicate your vegan needs. Some useful phrases for vegan travelers include:

"I am a vegan." (◇◇◇◇◇◇◇ - wǒ shì sù shí zhǔ yì zhě)

"I don't eat meat, dairy, or eggs." (◇◇◇◇◇◇◇◇◇◇◇ - wǒ bù chī ròu, rǔ zhì pǐn huò jī dàn)

"Is this dish vegan?" (◇◇◇◇◇◇◇◇ - zhè dào cài shì sù shí ma?)

Having these phrases handy can make it much easier to communicate your needs to waiters, chefs, and other locals, and will help you avoid accidentally eating non-vegan food.

Understanding Chinese Menu Labels:

When ordering food in China, it is also important to understand the labels and terminology used to describe different dishes. Some dishes may contain meat, dairy, or eggs even if they do not appear to do so based on their name or description. For example, some dishes that are labeled as "vegetable" may contain small amounts of meat or fish sauce. Additionally, some dishes that contain meat or eggs may be labeled as "vegetarian."

To avoid these misunderstandings, it is important to familiarize yourself with common Chinese menu labels and terminology, and to use your translation app to double-check the ingredients in a dish before ordering. Some common menu labels and terminology to look out for include:

"◇◇" (sù cài) - This label indicates that a dish is made with vegetables only, and does not contain meat, dairy, or eggs.

"◇◇" (sù shí) - This label indicates that a dish is vegetarian, but may contain dairy or eggs.

"◇◇◇◇◇" (sù shí zhǔ yì zhě) - This label indicates that a dish is suitable for vegans, and does not contain any animal products.

By understanding these labels and using your translation app to double-check, you can be confident that the food you order is suitable for your vegan diet.

In conclusion, using translation apps and understanding key phrases and menu labels can make a big difference when traveling as a vegan in China. With these tools, you can communicate your needs effectively and ensure that you have access to delicious and nutritious vegan food throughout your travels.

Staying Healthy as a Vegan in China

TRAVELING AS A VEGAN in a foreign country can be a unique challenge, particularly when it comes to finding nutritious and balanced meals. In China, where traditional cuisine is heavily centered around meat and dairy, this can be especially difficult. However, with a little planning and creativity, it is possible to maintain a healthy and balanced vegan diet while traveling in China.

Planning Meals in Advance:

Before you travel to China, it is a good idea to plan your meals in advance to ensure that you have access to healthy and nutritious vegan food. This can include researching restaurants and supermarkets that cater to vegans, and making a list of ingredients and dishes that you can easily find and prepare. Planning your meals ahead of time will also help you to avoid relying on junk food and processed snacks, which can be high in salt, sugar, and unhealthy fats.

Eating at Local Restaurants:

Eating at local restaurants can be a great way to experience the local cuisine, but it can also be a challenge for vegan travelers. To find restaurants that cater to vegans, it can be helpful to research online and read reviews from other travelers, or to look for restaurants that are labeled as "vegetarian" or "vegan." When dining out, be sure to use your translation app to communicate your needs, and to double-check the ingredients in a dish before ordering.

Shopping for Groceries:

Shopping for groceries can also be a great way to access healthy and nutritious vegan food while traveling in China. Supermarkets and local markets often offer a wide selection of fresh produce, including fruits, vegetables, grains, and legumes. These ingredients can be used to prepare simple and nutritious meals, such as salads, stir-fries, and soups. When shopping for groceries, it can also be helpful to familiarize yourself with common Chinese ingredients, such as tofu, tempeh, and miso, which are all excellent sources of plant-based protein.

Maintaining a Balanced Diet:

It is important to remember that a healthy and balanced vegan diet should include a variety of different foods from all the food groups, including fruits, vegetables, grains, legumes, and healthy fats. In China, it can be easy to rely on simple carbohydrates, such as rice and noodles, but it is important to include a variety of different foods to ensure that you are getting all the nutrients your body needs.

Staying Hydrated:

Staying hydrated is also important while traveling in China, especially during the hot and humid summer months. To stay hydrated, it is recommended to drink plenty of water throughout the day, and to avoid sugary drinks, such as soda and fruit juice, which can be high in added sugars.

In conclusion, by planning meals in advance, eating at local restaurants, shopping for groceries, maintaining a balanced diet, and staying hydrated, it is possible to maintain a healthy and nutritious vegan diet while traveling in China. With a little creativity and effort, you can have an enjoyable and fulfilling travel experience while staying true to your vegan principles.

Healthy Snack Options as a Vegan in China

SNACKS CAN PLAY AN important role in a healthy and balanced vegan diet, providing a quick source of energy and nutrients between meals. When traveling in China, it is important to choose snacks that are nutritious and satisfying, rather than relying on junk food or processed snacks that are high in salt, sugar, and unhealthy fats.

Fresh Fruits and Vegetables:

Fresh fruits and vegetables are an excellent choice for a healthy vegan snack in China. They are low in calories, high in fiber, and packed with vitamins, minerals, and antioxidants. Some popular fruits and vegetables in China include apples, bananas, pears, carrots, cucumbers, and tomatoes. These can be eaten raw, or added to smoothies and salads for a delicious and nutritious snack.

Nuts and Seeds:

Nuts and seeds are another great option for a healthy vegan snack in China. They are high in healthy fats, protein, and fiber, and can help to keep you feeling full and satisfied between meals. Some popular nuts and seeds in China include almonds, walnuts, pumpkin seeds, and sunflower seeds. These can be eaten raw, or added to granola, yogurt, or baked goods for a crunchy and nutritious snack.

Plant-Based Snacks:

There are also a number of plant-based snacks available in China that are suitable for vegans, including crackers, rice cakes, and dried fruits. These can be found at supermarkets and health food stores, and can be a great option for when you are on the go and need a quick and convenient snack.

Street Food:

Street food can be a fun and delicious way to experience the local cuisine, but it is important to be careful when choosing vegan-friendly options. Some street foods in China, such as steamed buns and dumplings, can be made with animal-based ingredients, so it is important to check the ingredients before purchasing. On the other hand, there are also street foods that are vegan-friendly, such as steamed vegetables and rice cakes, which can be a great option for a quick and tasty snack.

Packaged Snacks:

There are also a number of packaged snacks available in China that are suitable for vegans, including trail mix, protein bars, and dark chocolate. These can be found at supermarkets and health food stores, and can be a great option for when you are on the go and need a quick and convenient snack.

In conclusion, there are many healthy and delicious snack options available for vegans in China, including fresh fruits and vegetables, nuts and seeds, plant-based snacks, street food, and packaged snacks. With a little creativity and effort, it is possible to enjoy a variety of nutritious and satisfying snacks while traveling in China.

Eating Vegan Street Food in China

STREET FOOD IS AN INTEGRAL part of Chinese culture, and provides a unique and delicious way to experience the local cuisine. For vegans, street food can also be a great way to find quick and convenient vegan-friendly options when traveling in China. However, it is important to be cautious when choosing street food, as many street foods in China can contain animal-based ingredients, such as meat, dairy, and eggs.

Research Before You Go:

Before heading out to try street food in China, it is a good idea to research popular vegan-friendly options and learn some basic phrases in Chinese to communicate with vendors. This can help to ensure that you are able to find vegan-friendly street foods that meet your dietary requirements and preferences. Some popular vegan street foods in China include steamed buns filled with vegetables, fried rice with tofu, and stir-fried noodles with vegetables.

LOOK FOR VEGAN-FRIENDLY Stalls:

When trying street food in China, look for stalls that offer a variety of vegan-friendly options, and are used to accommodating vegans. Some street food stalls in China have separate cooking equipment and utensils for vegetarian and vegan dishes, which can help to reduce the risk of cross-contamination.

Ask Questions:

It is important to communicate with vendors and ask questions about the ingredients used in their street foods. This can help to ensure that the food you are eating is vegan-friendly and free from animal-based ingredients. Some common questions to ask include "does this contain meat or dairy?", "are there any eggs in this dish?" and "is this cooked with any animal-based sauces?"

Be Prepared:

When trying street food in China, it is a good idea to bring along a water bottle, a hand sanitizer, and some tissues. This can help to ensure that you are able to stay hydrated and clean while eating on the go. Additionally, it is also a good idea to bring along a small bag or backpack to store your street food, as well as any other essentials you may need, such as a camera or a phone.

In conclusion, street food can be a fun and delicious way to experience the local cuisine while traveling in China. By researching popular vegan-friendly options, looking for vegan-friendly stalls, asking questions, and being prepared, it is possible to enjoy a variety of tasty and nutritious street foods while staying true to your vegan diet.

Chapter 7: Bonus Vegan Recipes

Mapo Tofu:

INGREDIENTS:

    1 block (14 oz) of silken tofu
    2 tablespoons vegetable oil
    2 cloves of garlic, minced
    1 inch piece of ginger, minced
    2 green onions, thinly sliced
    2 tablespoons fermented black bean paste
    2 tablespoons doubanjiang (spicy bean paste)

1 tablespoon Sichuan peppercorns

1 cup water

1 teaspoon cornstarch mixed with 1 tablespoon water

Salt to taste

Optional: 1 cup chopped vegetables (such as bell peppers, mushrooms, or bok choy)

Instructions:

Cut the tofu into bite-sized cubes and set aside.

Heat the vegetable oil in a wok or large frying pan over medium-high heat. Add the garlic, ginger, and green onions and stir-fry for 1-2 minutes until fragrant.

Add the fermented black bean paste, doubanjiang, and Sichuan peppercorns and continue to stir-fry for another minute.

Add the water and optional vegetables and bring to a boil. Reduce heat and let simmer for 5-7 minutes.

Carefully add the tofu to the pan, being careful not to break the cubes. Let cook for 2-3 minutes until heated through.

Slowly add the cornstarch mixture, stirring continuously, until the sauce thickens. Season with salt to taste.

Serve the Mapo Tofu over steamed rice and garnish with additional sliced green onions, if desired. Enjoy!

Note: This recipe can be adjusted to your desired level of spiciness by adding or reducing the amount of doubanjiang and Sichuan peppercorns.

Buddha's Delight:

INGREDIENTS:
    1 cup dried shiitake mushrooms
    1 cup dried lily buds
    1 cup glass noodles
    1 cup julienned carrots
    1 cup julienned bamboo shoots
    1 cup julienned bell peppers
    1 cup julienned snow peas
    1 tablespoon vegetable oil
    2 cloves of garlic, minced
    2 inches of ginger, minced
    2 green onions, thinly sliced
    3 cups vegetable broth
    2 tablespoons soy sauce
    1 tablespoon hoisin sauce
    1 teaspoon sugar

Salt and pepper to taste

Instructions:

Soak the dried shiitake mushrooms and lily buds in separate bowls with warm water for 30 minutes, or until softened. Drain and set aside.

Soak the glass noodles in warm water for 5-10 minutes, or until softened. Drain and set aside.

Heat the vegetable oil in a wok or large frying pan over medium-high heat. Add the garlic, ginger, and green onions and stir-fry for 1-2 minutes until fragrant.

Add the soaked shiitake mushrooms, lily buds, carrots, bamboo shoots, bell peppers, and snow peas to the pan and continue to stir-fry for 2-3 minutes.

Add the vegetable broth, soy sauce, hoisin sauce, and sugar to the pan and bring to a boil. Reduce heat and let simmer for 5-7 minutes, or until the vegetables are tender.

Add the softened glass noodles to the pan and continue to cook for another 2-3 minutes, or until heated through.

Season with salt and pepper to taste. Serve the Buddha's Delight over steamed rice and garnish with additional sliced green onions, if desired. Enjoy!

Note: You can also add other ingredients to this dish, such as tempeh, tofu, or seitan, to make it more substantial. Feel free to experiment with different vegetables and flavorings to make it your own.

Ma Po Bean Curd

INGREDIENTS:

1 block (14 oz) of firm tofu

2 tablespoons vegetable oil

2 cloves of garlic, minced

1 inch piece of ginger, minced

2 green onions, thinly sliced

2 tablespoons fermented black bean paste

2 tablespoons doubanjiang (spicy bean paste)

1 tablespoon Sichuan peppercorns

1 cup water

1 teaspoon cornstarch mixed with 1 tablespoon water

Salt to taste

Optional: 1 cup chopped vegetables (such as bell peppers, mushrooms, or bok choy)

Instructions:

Cut the tofu into bite-sized cubes and set aside.

Heat the vegetable oil in a wok or large frying pan over medium-high heat. Add the garlic, ginger, and green onions and stir-fry for 1-2 minutes until fragrant.

Add the fermented black bean paste, doubanjiang, and Sichuan peppercorns and continue to stir-fry for another minute.

Add the water and optional vegetables and bring to a boil. Reduce heat and let simmer for 5-7 minutes.

Carefully add the tofu to the pan, being careful not to break the cubes. Let cook for 2-3 minutes until heated through.

Slowly add the cornstarch mixture, stirring continuously, until the sauce thickens. Season with salt to taste.

Serve the Ma Po Bean Curd over steamed rice and garnish with additional sliced green onions, if desired. Enjoy!

Note: This recipe can be adjusted to your desired level of spiciness by adding or reducing the amount of doubanjiang and Sichuan peppercorns.

Zhajiangmian

INGREDIENTS:

8 oz fresh Chinese wheat noodles or udon noodles

1 tablespoon vegetable oil

2 cloves of garlic, minced

1 inch piece of ginger, minced

2 green onions, thinly sliced

1 cup diced shiitake mushrooms

1 cup diced carrots

1 cup diced zucchini

1 cup diced bell peppers

1 cup diced tofu

1/2 cup zhajiang (fermented soybean paste)

1/2 cup water

1 tablespoon soy sauce

1 teaspoon sugar

Salt and pepper to taste

Instructions:

Cook the noodles according to package instructions. Drain and set aside.

Heat the vegetable oil in a wok or large frying pan over medium-high heat. Add the garlic, ginger, and green onions and stir-fry for 1-2 minutes until fragrant.

Add the shiitake mushrooms, carrots, zucchini, bell peppers, and tofu and continue to stir-fry for 2-3 minutes, or until the vegetables are slightly softened.

Add the zhajiang, water, soy sauce, and sugar to the pan and stir to combine. Bring to a boil, then reduce heat and let simmer for 5-7 minutes.

Serve the Zhajiangmian by dividing the cooked noodles into bowls and spooning the sauce over the top. Sprinkle with salt and pepper to taste. Enjoy!

Note: Feel free to experiment with different vegetables and flavorings to make this dish your own. Zhajiangmian is a versatile dish that can be customized to your taste preferences.

Sticky Rice Wrapped in Lotus Leaves:

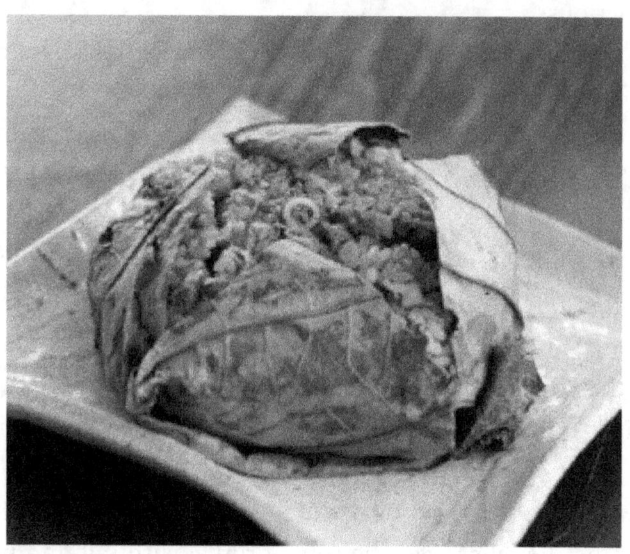

INGREDIENTS:

    2 cups glutinous (sticky) rice
    1/2 cup chopped shiitake mushrooms
    1/2 cup diced carrots
    1/2 cup diced water chestnuts
    1/2 cup diced bamboo shoots
    1/4 cup diced scallions
    2 tablespoons soy sauce
    1 tablespoon hoisin sauce
    1 tablespoon sesame oil
    1 teaspoon sugar
    Salt and pepper to taste
    8 dried lotus leaves, soaked in warm water for 1 hour
    Kitchen twine
    Instructions:

Rinse the sticky rice and soak it in water for 30 minutes. Drain and set aside.

In a large bowl, mix together the shiitake mushrooms, carrots, water chestnuts, bamboo shoots, scallions, soy sauce, hoisin sauce, sesame oil, sugar, salt, and pepper.

Lay a lotus leaf on a flat surface and place a portion of the sticky rice (about 1/2 cup) in the center of the leaf. Spoon a portion of the vegetable mixture (about 1/4 cup) on top of the rice.

Fold the sides of the lotus leaf up and over the filling, and then roll the leaf up from one end to the other, sealing the filling inside. Repeat with the remaining lotus leaves and filling.

Tie each parcel with kitchen twine to secure the filling inside.

Place a steaming basket in a large pot of boiling water and place the parcels in the basket. Cover the pot and steam for 20-25 minutes, or until the rice is fully cooked and the filling is heated through.

Serve the sticky rice parcels hot and enjoy the fragrant and savory flavor of the lotus leaves.

Note: You can also wrap other fillings, such as diced chicken or pork, to suit your preferences. Enjoy experimenting with different flavors and ingredients to create your own unique variation of this traditional dish!

Conclusion

China is a country that truly embraces its rich culinary heritage and offers a wealth of vegan options for travelers. From the bustling street food markets to traditional home-style cooking, the country is a vegan's paradise, with a wealth of flavors and textures to explore. For those who are concerned about language barriers, translation apps and a few key phrases can make it easy to communicate dietary restrictions and find vegan-friendly options.

One of the most exciting aspects of vegan travel in China is discovering the many delicious and nutritious snacks that are available. Whether it's munching on juicy sweet and savory street-side fruit, or indulging in traditional vegan treats like sticky rice parcels and Buddha's Delight, there are countless options to keep you fueled and satisfied throughout your travels.

For those who are interested in staying healthy, there are many ways to ensure that your vegan diet is balanced and nourishing. From incorporating fresh produce and whole grains into your meals, to exploring the many plant-based protein options available in the country, it is possible to stay healthy and feel your best while you explore this amazing country.

In addition to the incredible food, China is also a culturally rich country, with a long and fascinating history. By visiting temples and shrines, vegans can learn more about the local customs and beliefs, while discovering some of the country's most beautiful and historic landmarks. Whether you're drawn to the bustling cityscapes or prefer to wander the serene countryside, there's something for everyone in this fascinating country.

In conclusion, "Discovering Vegan China" has shown that this incredible country is not just a destination for food lovers, but also a destination for those who seek adventure, cultural immersion, and a healthy, fulfilling lifestyle. With its rich food culture and abundance of delicious, healthy, and sustainable options, there's never been a better time to explore the vegan side of China. Whether you're traveling for business or for pleasure, you're sure to leave with memories that will last a lifetime.

Resources for continued learning.

WEBSITES: THERE ARE several websites dedicated to veganism in China, including "Happy Cow" and "Vegan China," which list vegan-friendly restaurants and cafes, as well as resources for finding vegan products and ingredients.

Social media: Follow vegan influencers and food bloggers on platforms like Instagram and Weibo to stay updated on the latest vegan trends and news in China.

Online communities: Join online vegan communities, such as Facebook groups or forums, to connect with other vegans and share tips, recipes, and experiences.

Books: There are a number of books available that focus on veganism in China, including "The Vegan's Guide to China" and "Vegan China: A Guide to the Best Food, Drinks, and Markets." These books offer comprehensive guides to navigating the country as a vegan, as well as recipes, tips, and recommendations.

Cooking classes: Consider taking a cooking class to learn more about traditional Chinese vegan cooking. Classes can be found in larger cities, such as Beijing and Shanghai, and are a great way to get hands-on experience with cooking local dishes.

Local events: Look for local events, such as food festivals and cooking workshops, that showcase vegan-friendly options and provide opportunities to learn more about the cuisine and culture of China.

These resources can help continue your journey of learning about veganism in China, and help you explore this amazing country to its fullest potential.

YouTube channels: There are many YouTube channels dedicated to veganism and cooking, including channels that focus on veganism in China. These channels offer cooking tutorials, recipe demonstrations, and tips for eating vegan in the country.

Food Tours: Join a food tour specifically focused on vegan options in China. These tours are led by experienced guides and offer a great opportunity to learn more about local food culture and sample a variety of vegan dishes.

Chinese Language Learning: Learning basic Mandarin can help in communicating dietary restrictions and finding vegan options in the country. Consider taking a language class or using online resources such as Duolingo or Babbel.

Volunteer opportunities: Volunteer at local vegan organizations, such as animal sanctuaries or community gardens, to gain hands-on experience and learn more about the local vegan community.

Cultural Activities: Participate in cultural activities, such as tea ceremonies, to gain a deeper understanding of the country's traditions and values. Many traditional Chinese activities, such as tea ceremonies, are vegan-friendly.

These additional resources provide opportunities to deepen your understanding of veganism in China, while also gaining a deeper appreciation for the country's rich culture and cuisine.

About the Author

My name is Rami and I am passionate about promoting the benefits of a vegan lifestyle through delicious and easy-to-make recipes, as well as tips and advice on how to incorporate a vegan lifestyle into your daily routine.

I became vegan for ethical, environmental, and health reasons, and I believe that a plant-based diet can improve the lives of both people and animals. On my books, you'll find a variety of vegan recipes that are not only delicious, but also easy to make. From breakfast to dinner and everything in between, my recipes are perfect for anyone looking to try veganism or to add more plant-based meals to their diet.

In addition to recipes, I will also be sharing tips and advice on how to make the transition to a vegan lifestyle as smooth as possible. Whether it's advice on finding vegan options when eating out, or suggestions for

cruelty-free beauty and household products, I want to make it as easy as possible for you to live a compassionate and sustainable lifestyle.
I believe that a vegan diet and lifestyle can be delicious, varied, and easy to follow. I am constantly experimenting with new ingredients and techniques to create unique and delicious dishes that will inspire you to try veganism.
I hope you will join me on this journey of discovery and experimentation and will find my books helpful in your quest to live a more compassionate, healthy, and sustainable life.

Don't miss out!

Visit the website below and you can sign up to receive emails whenever Rami Georgiev publishes a new book. There's no charge and no obligation.

https://books2read.com/r/B-A-JXNW-SNGFC

BOOKS 2 READ

Connecting independent readers to independent writers.

Also by Rami Georgiev

The Ultimate Vegan European Recipe Book - From the Streets of Paris
to the Beaches of Greece
The Vegan Mindset: Living a Compassionate and Conscious Life
Vegan Beauty Made Easy
Vegan Parenting: Raising the Next Generation of Earth Stewards
Roaming for a Better World:
The Plant-Powered Athlete
Discovering Vegan India
The Path to Enlightenment
Karma in Action
Discovering Vegan France
Conversation with the Devil
Discovering Vegan China
Vegan Paradise in Bali
Discovering Vegan Italy:
Psychology Facts: How to Read People's Minds.
Unmasking the Shadows: Exploring the Depths of Dark Psychology
Confidence Unleashed
The Power of Words
The Silent Conversation: Mastering the Art of Body Language
The Conscious Connection: Unlocking the Secrets to Mindful
Relationships
Mindful Mastery
The Subconscious Mastery Blueprint

Embracing the Unvarnished Truth: 40 Truths About Human
Relationships
Forty Paths to Happiness: Embrace Transformation, Leave the Past
Behind, and Discover Joyful Living
The Art of Mind Reading: 40 Techniques for Unveiling Thoughts and
Motivations
Stress Management: 35 Transformative Techniques to Prevent and
Reduce Everyday Stress in Your Life
Transforming Habits: 40 Proven Strategies to Cultivate Positive Change
in Your Life

Watch for more at vegandelights.space.